Without Dragons Even the Emperor Would Be Lonely

Ninso John High

Ensos, Parables & Koans

Wet Cement Press
Berkeley, California

Copyright© 2020 John High
All rights reserved

ISBN: 978-1-7324369-4-7

Wet Cement Press
Berkeley, California
www.wetcementpress.com

Cover image: Ninso John High

Acknowledgments:
After doing a workshop with the great Japanese calligrapher, Kazuaki Tanahashi, I asked if he would paint an enso for my book. He stared at me for a long time. Then, he said—No, do it yourself. Thank you, Kaz.

WCP8-5
Second Edition

Contents

Epigraph • 7
Koans
    Book One • 9
Parables
    One • 21
    Two • 29
    Three • 35
    Four • 41
    Five • 47
Dragon Ensos
    Dragon Blood • 60
    Slow Dance Dragons • 61
    Without Dragons Even the Emperor Would Be Lonely • 62
    Patience Winter Dragons • 63
Parables
    Six • 65
    Seven • 75
    Eight • 87
    Nine • 97
    Ten • 105
    Eleven • 119
Koans
    Book Two • 133
About the Author • 149

It is the page that speaks. The words are alive. A whiteness of scrolls pulling a being toward the sea. Just as you in this moment's passing, the sea lingers in a word & voice between the light & dark. This is no other than who we are.

The boy's journal

Koans
Book One

FROM SCROLL XVI:

IN THE KOAN, THE MAN IS WALKING TOO, DO YOU REMEMBER?

I REMEMBER, YES.

THE LOST CHILDREN ARE WALKING TOO, FOLLOWING YOU NOW IN THE DREAM.

WHY WOULD THEY FOLLOW ME?

DREAMS ARE WORDS.
SO YOU SIP THE TEA.
FINISH THE CUP.
WHEN YOU SIP THIS TEA,
YOU DRINK THE SEA.

THE BODY SPEAKS.
WHEN YOU HEAR IT, YOU
AWAKEN IN THE DREAM.
AND THE DREAM VANISHES.
THEN WE CAN TRAVEL
  IN THE DREAM WORLD FREELY.
FREEING OTHERS.
  FREEDOM IS NONE OTHER
THAN THIS.

THE WORLD IS NOT
  WHAT THE WORLD IS,
IT IS WHAT YOU ARE.

LOOK, SOMEONE IS WAITING
     FOR YOU.

No wound,
 no wounder,
 no woundedness....

We have no language
 for this,
 so the word chosen
 for the scrolls
 is infinite.

(The boy's diary)

Do not be distracted by death. Finish it.

In these stars that go nameless in the sea.

As if awakened
 from a dream
& falling into
 your own arms
what took you so long?

— Lou Hartman

JUST WHEN I THOUGHT
    HE COULDN'T GO ON,
THERE WE ALL ARE.

Parable One

THE BOY PLUNGES INTO THE HAND
   & THE HAND SPEAKS. THE SEA SWAYING
   IN THE SKY & THE BRUSH TETTERING
      ON THE EDGE OF A HAND.
YOU THINK YOU KNOW WHAT IT MEANS,
     AND YOU NEVER NEEDED TO KNOW—
   A SEA MIRACULOUS IN ITS OWN LANGUAGE.

& translating itself without words. A mango tree hearing the sound of brush. So many hours in this place and the dead calming, listening to the girl's lips moving by the pagoda. A dog

SLEEPING BY A STONE DRAGON
NEAR THE GATE OF PRAYERS.
THE BOY THINKS — THIS IS AN INK
DRAWING I WILL FIND WHEN
I GET OLD. HE SMELLS THE WHISTLE
OF THE CICADA FROM THE FOREST
& MOVES THE HAND ACROSS THE
PAGE. AND FOR A MOMENT
•THERE IS °NO SOUND.

Parable Two

Once while you were sleeping you heard the trains arriving. Or were these departures from the old station. There was only one track tracing through the countryside & the stations themselves were without names. If there were passangers along the way, you only saw

REFLECTIONS OF
THEIR FACES THROUGH
THE WINDOWS.
THOUGH AT ONE TIME, IT IS TRUE,
THEY HAD NAMES & PLACES, YOU ARE
CERTAIN. AND SOMEWHERE IN THE SLEEPING,
THERE WERE ONCE COUNTRIES, OR NATIONS,
OR STRUMMING   OF A GUITAR —
OR PERHAPS JUST A VIBRATION
AT EACH STATION. THERE WERE SO
MANY MIGRATIONS YOU OFTEN
WONDERED WHERE YOU WERE, OR EVEN
WHO YOU WERE WHEN YOUR TRAIN

Pulled into the station. Some were great cities, and others villages or towns, some too distant to describe. Yet there were mountains & rivers along the track, and at times, there were populations & buildings too immense to recall. You remember the remembering most. Its territory of skies & a constant humming along the tracks, in the faces, in the windows & doorways. Looking out as you see all this, and it is as close as the voices you hear in the humming; almost like hymns, or

some human choir.

Parable Three

It was the man by the mouth of the river who wrote the letter. His body like faded stones

aged water. You had waited for him a long time. Yet now you were unsure. Were you waiting for him, or was he waiting for you? Somehow, he and his dog brought you here. You recalled following the path along the river to the sea. The egrits & gulls guiding when

YOU WERE LOST. THE BOY
WITH ONE EYE, AND THE GIRL
SPEAKING IN SIGNS. WHOLE
YEARS PASSED, AS IF SLEEPING
THROUGH A MOVIE, A MIRROR
OF SHIFTING FACES IN THE
WATER'S CURRENT. WHILE
RESTING IN THE SHADE OF
A EUCALYPTUS & WASHING
YOUR SHIRT, YOU SAW
A CHILD PEEKING THROUGH
THE MANGO. OR WAS
THAT ONLY ANOTHER
FACE FROM
THE RIVER ?

THERE IS NO
WAY OF TELLING
WHO IS WHO, OR WHO IS YOU.
STILL, YOU RECOGNIZED THE MOUTH
& EYES, AS ONLY YOU COULD. IT WAS NOT
HARD FOR YOU TO UNDERSTAND WHERE
SHE CAME FROM AS SHE HANDED YOU
THE LETTER. HER SWAYING LIKE SALT
IN THE SEA. IT WAS THE OLD MAN WHO
WROTE THE LETTER. THOUGH IT IS TRUE
YOU COULD NOT YET DECIPHER

THE WORDS. AN ALPHABET YOU STILL COULDN'T BEGIN TO REMEMBER. BUT WHEN WAS THAT, HOW LONG HAD IT TAKEN YOU TO ARRIVE? YOU CAN TRUST THE ROAD IS ALL YOU COULD HEAR FROM THE WIND COMING OUT OF HER MOUTH, OR WAS IT HER HANDS? YOU ARE THE ROAD IS ALL YOU CAN EVER REMEMBER....

Parable Four

Another time while you were walking you spotted a tree on a rooftop. The mid-day sun relentless, still a breeze blowing about the boy's feet. You were studying him from the road

along the river, among
the mockingbirds & frogs
who seemed to have province
in these fields. You were
preparing to disappear, or
vanish — is there a difference —
when you suddenly eyed
the tree on the rooftop
of an abandoned pagoda.
But then, it may not
be abandoned you thought,
for there was the boy

perhaps dancing in the field.
Or at least it appeared the breeze
came from the kicking in the air
of his feet. It reached your
parched face —

though he
was quite a
ways in
the distance,
and all of
the folliage
& grasses
abouts were
utterly still.

There were both mango & banana trees,
yet even they appeared almost human. And

That's when you saw the girl
come out on the roof, walk over to the tree,
and wave to you. She cupped her hands around
her mouth & for a second you imagined she
was calling to you. You could even make out
the movement of her lips, but could
hear nothing. Though the boy

was running now,
running as fast
as he could
to the pagoda.

Parable Five

When you arrived at the station
of the dead, things were different than
you expected. It's always the same — things
are different than you think. It makes you think
about thinking or what it is. Are the dead
at this station really dead, for instance? As
far as your eyes can see, nothing looks
like what you see is dead. Or is it what
you don't see that makes you think
this is a station for the dead or that

is only more thinking while not
thinking about thinking. Where are all
the ghosts & spirits — or zombies you
heard about from films you were too
frightened to watch? You remember
the boy scared in his room by
monsters at night. You wanted
nothing of that. Still, here
you are at the station
of the dead — the sky an
almost crimson blue.

the frame of the archway. You find
no ticketmaster or conductor.
Tracks run along an orchard &
on into the rice paddies to a town,
or perhaps a large village off over
the horizon. So what does it mean, these
children giggling in the school yard—
you can hear their voices, though you
cannot yet translate their language— &

WHAT ABOUT THE WHISPERS & CLAMOR —
MORE LAUGHTER, YES — YOU CAN MAKE
THAT OUT OK — SLIPPING BETWEEN THE
DOORWAYS & WINDOWS OF HOUSES,
OR HUTS. AND THE GIRL WITH HER
MOTHER WITHOUT FAMILIAR FACES
WHO JUST HANDED YOU A GLASS OF GINGER

WATER? YOU MAY WONDER
WHAT IT MEANS, YET SOMEHOW
YOU UNDERSTAND YOU'LL NEVER KNOW.
STILL, YOU HAVE BEEN HERE & THAT
IS ENOUGH. NO ONE IS BOTHERED BY
YOUR ARRIVALS OR DEPARTURES.
AND YOU SENSE IT HAS ALWAYS
BEEN LIKE THIS, BOW & WAVE TO
THE UNNAMED & BOARD ANOTHER
TRAIN AS YOU PASS ALONG THE
WAY IN THE BOOK OF CHANGES.

Dragon Ensos

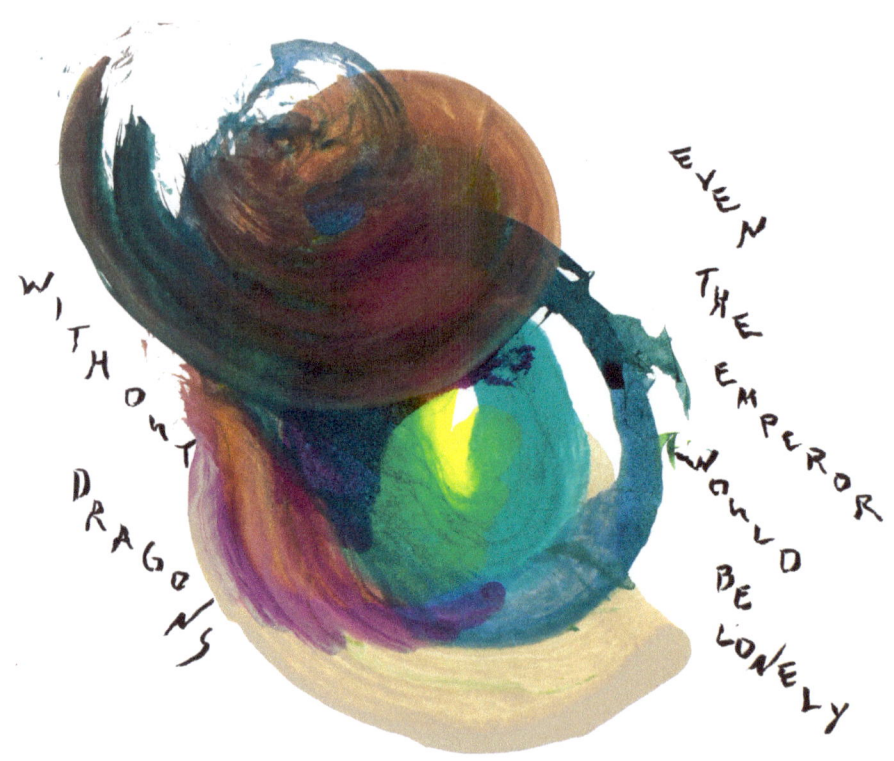

Parable Six

When you woke up you
were on a beach looking out
on small fishing boats. The mountains
& hills lifting from the sea, a darker
green than you remembered. The boats —
of a time before you were born. You
recalled the sound of a radio, the
projector of the film booth. Though
there was no evidence of their

existence among the white sand.
Driftwood bobbing in the sea. Yet
it is possible this was another person
You couldn't say for sure. The palm &
willow spread among pineapple & mango
trees — breathing? (You may be inventing
this, as in memory of an old film.) Just
the sound of breeze in leaves & new
waves. Here, the boy & girl strolling

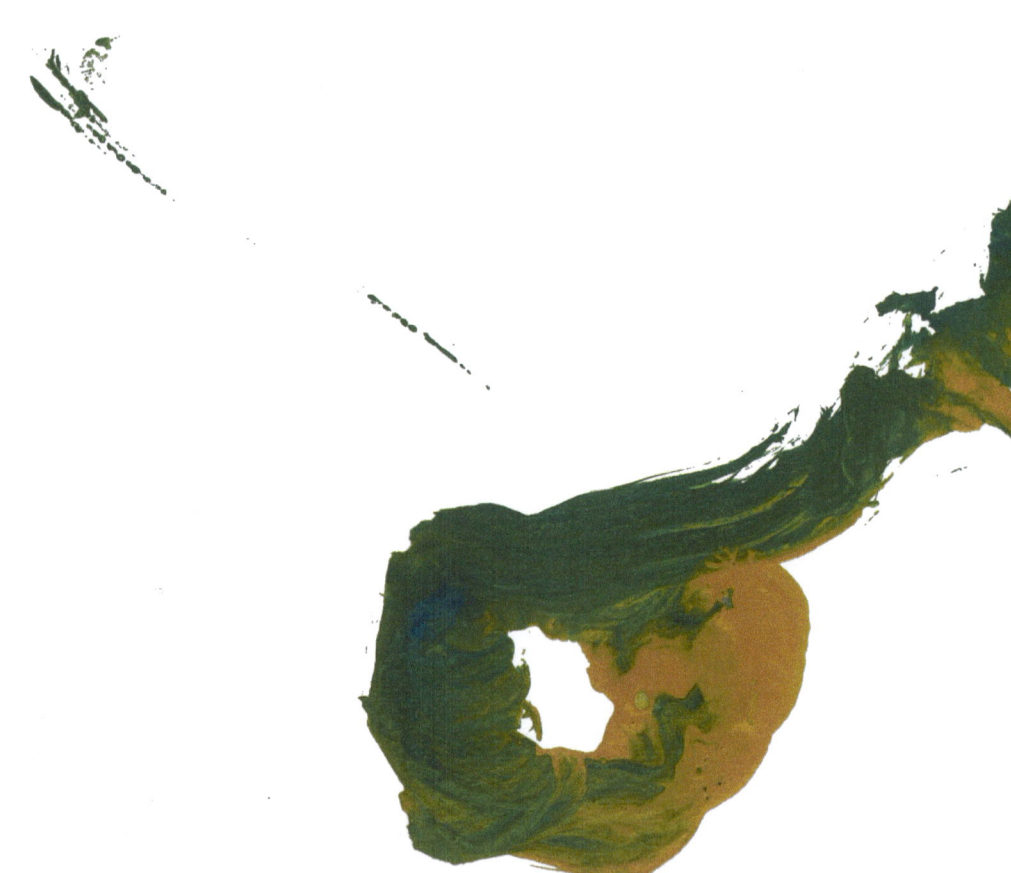

down the beach doesn't startle
you. You might even report you
were glad of their presence. Without
them you may even be lonely, or at
the least, without a companion.
After all, how had you awoken

on this shore, and where had you
laid down & fallen asleep
 the night before? Yet you
sense no resolve to resolve
 this question as you take
off your shirt &
 wander into the very
blue & green water,

# Parable Seven

WHILE drifting out on sea,
   the faces of the fish appeared
  happy. In any case, these fish
   couldn't be dead, or you
    had misunderstood everything
     right from the beginning.
       Pools of minnows & albacore
         intermingling together.
       The coral a light sparkling
          on fins, the sun carrying

you down. But this had nothing
to do with drowning. Coming
up for air these beauties
followed, floating across
the crest of small waves &
gliding along the body. As
you grew nearer the first
mountain — maybe we should call it
an island, or forested hill — it lifted
up by the current or tide & there

you spotted some tents, what looked like
tents scattered about a quite small temple.
WITH CURIOUS CARVINGS. These carvings apparently
SCULPTED into the green & brown stone of
a shrine. It was too hard to make out
the figures, but for a moment you could swear
these figures were dancing & that a whole
population of trees swayed in a kind of
set rhythm. The water mild & translascent,
even pleasant on the skin — was it your
skin — as you glimpsed

the fishing boats where all
these shadows you couldn't
make out were tossing husks
of bread to the fish. The
fish now surfacing about
the hulls of wooden boats
the same color as the sea you
were leaving. Then you heard the voices

OF TREES & you thought they were your own childhoods gathering in the white sand of the shore. Were they really you, or who you had once been?

Parable Eight

BACK STROKING TO SHORE, THE FISHING BOATS
WITHOUT FISHERMEN FOLLOWED YOU. AS
DID THE MINNOWS & ALBACORE, SOME FISH
YOU'D NEVER SEEN BEFORE, BUT YOU
ODDLY RECOGNIZED THE FOUR SEALS
THAT FANNED OUT ALONG THE COASTLINE
IN A NEARLY PERFECT LINE OF
LATERAL FORMATION. THIS IMPRESSION
THEY WERE TALKING — TO YOU — THOUGH
YOU SUSPECTED THIS WAS JUST THE FLUTTERS
OF FALLING LEAVES FROM THE MANGO

TREES. THERE WAS THE FOREST JUST BEYOND THE WHITE SANDS & PAGODA. STILL, WHEN YOU TURNED BACK TO LOOK AGAIN, THE WOODEN BOATS & FISH BOBBED IN THE WAVES NEAR YOUR FEET. AS IF IN A CONVERSATION OF THEIR OWN. THE STONE FIGURES CARVED INTO THE PAGODA WALLS ON THE HILLS TO YOUR LEFT & RIGHT. THOUGH THEY WERE APPARENTLY INANIMATE, YOU SUDDENLY UNDERSTOOD

YOU HAD NEVER BEEN ALONE.
SWAYING PAPAYA BRANCHES IN THE TREES
ALONG THIS HORIZON. CICADAS &
MOCKING BIRDS, NOT VISIBLE TO THE EYE,
AS IF THEY WERE YOUR OWN EYES
HEARING, PERHAPS CREATING, YOU
IN THAT MOMENT. THE PAST & FUTURE
VANISHED BEFORE YOU COULD DISCERN
WHAT WAS HAPPENING. THIS, AS BEST
YOU COULD TELL, CAUSED YOU TO WANDER

back in time to another life & place, you thought of all the friends & families you had known and wished them well, certain you would meet again. Then you bowed & entered the temple, no longer remembering your name and without any notion, or desire, to do so.

Parable Nine

As you were departing the island,
   a fisherwoman in the fishing boats
suddenly appeared. A body's embrace of
   water when you spotted the waving
by the shoreline. Already the terrain
   of the pagoda slipping back, a sparkle of
turquois mirroring from the stone dragons'
   architecture, reaching its way back
into the water that stretched out &
   beyond the boats floating willfully,
you sensed this, like moving maps,
   on an immense sea. Though true

You had no idea where they were going — much less where you would go — & it seemed these figures were ready to carry you on their backs above the water. Yet surely, you thought, this must be an act of their imagination.

The mute girl & one-eyed boy already on a boat, casting nets into the waves as the fish that accompanied you earlier

swam about, as if wanting to enter & play around in the nets that could not catch them. A choral sounding of whose voices from the reefs? Perhaps the trees in some form of echoing — O Captain, my Captain — & then remembering you had heard the voice as a boy, and it was this leading you on in a return to the world of language.

Parable Ten

THERE WAS THE WINTER
    AHEAD — & THE WINTER BEHIND —
 & SOON YOU WOULD WALK AGAIN
    IN THE SNOW. THE MANGO TREES
 IN A GROVE. THE GRAVEL PATH
    INTO THE RICE PADDIES.
 A STATION HERE, A TRAIN
    THERE, AND YESTERDAY'S

SEA ALREADY A MEMORY
OF REMEMBERING. AND WHO
WAS THE UNDYING PERSON
IN THE WAVES? THE BOY & GIRL
ON A WOODEN BOAT. THOSE FISH
INNUMERABLE AS THE WHITE
SANDS. DID YOU REALLY THINK
IT MEANT SOMETHING OTHER

than this? You have left the trains and the fisher women who brought you here. But do you even know where that is? So many questions as you walk by the school yard. So many passengers dispersing along the

ROADS. THE QUESTION QUESTIONS
THE QUESTION, APPEARS & DISAPPEARS.
THE RIPE BANANAS THESE VILLAGERS
NEAR THE STATION SHARED WITH YOU.
THERE WAS A TIME YOU NEEDED
TO KNOW FROM BOTH THE LIVING

& THE DEAD. TODAY
THE SKY SEAMLESS,
 THE NOT KNOWING,
 PERHAPS, MORE INTIMATE?
  THE SEEN & UNSEEN
  MERGING TOGETHER
  AS YOU REJOIN

THE WORLD a WORD WITH
ALL THE WALKERS, TALKING &
GOING WHEREVER IT IS THEY
GO. IT IS ENOUGH, YOU THINK,
ENOUGH TO BE ALIVE RIGHT HERE.

Parable Eleven

JUST AS YOU ARE ABOUT TO CLOSE
THE BOOK AND SIGN THE PAGES THE GIRL
IN A CHECKERED UNIFORM HANDED
YOU A SHEAF WITH WRAPPED SCROLLS.
THEY WERE ROLLED NEATLY IN A
BAMBOO BINDER, THE THICKNESS
OF THE PAPER CRISP, AS IF EACH
PAGE HAD BEEN HAND CUT, ALMOST

LIKE THE DARK BARK
FROM A FIG TREE — THE SMELL
OF BURNT LEAVES. YOU INSTINCTIVELY
SENSED IT WAS FOR THE LETTER YOU
WOULD WRITE TO YOURSELF TO OPEN
IN 25 YEARS FOR THE MAN AT
THE MOUTH OF THE RIVER WITH
A BODY OF THAT OF FADED
STONES, AGED WATER. YOU NOW

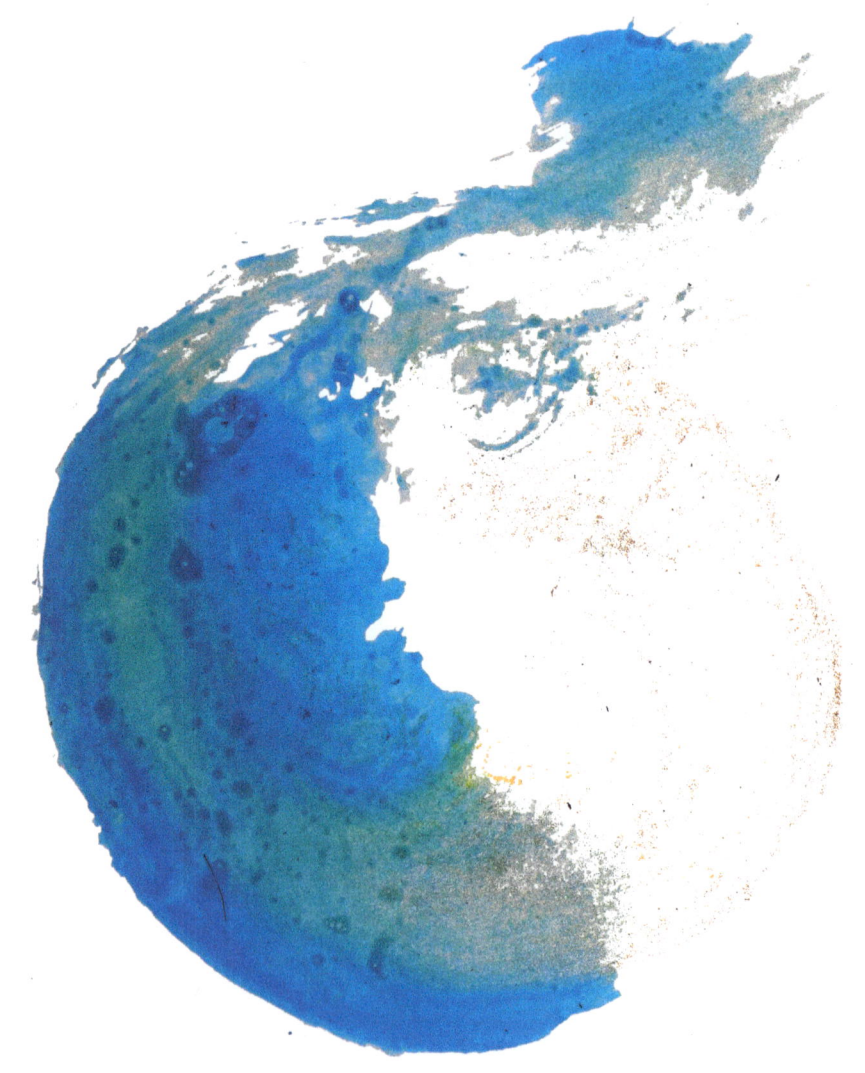

recalled eyeing him as you
passed along the road, resting
on the bank, confused, lost some
where, though you couldn't put
your finger on exactly where
or when. And now here was the
same girl, mute you had once
thought — yet how was her voice
speaking, or translating

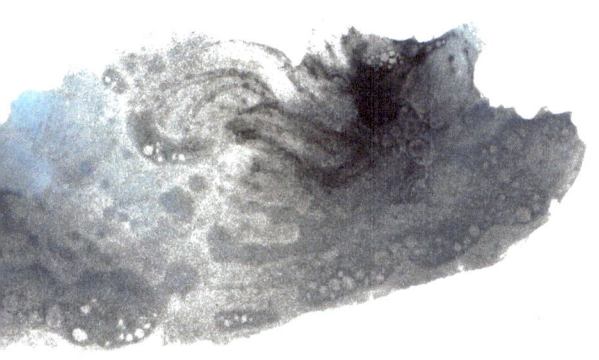

THE WORDS IN A SOUND AUDIBLE,
AT LEAST SO IT SEEMED TO YOU,
FROM THE MOVEMENT OF HER HANDS?
HERE SHE WAS AGAIN IN A BLACK & WHITE
CHECKERED DRESS, IT DIDN'T REALLY
MATTER TO YOU HOW YOU COULD HEAR HER
VOICE, ONLY THAT YOU COULD HEAR HER
AGAIN, AS YOU TURNED TO THANK HER,
YOU SAW THE ONE-EYED BOY HAD JOINED

her under a miraculous sky.
The boy, too, clad in a school
uniform, black & white, barefoot
as was she, nodding his head.
Uncertain as to the appropriate
response, you skimmed through
the blank pages. There was nothing
left for you to do than to

WRITE THE LETTER. BUT WHAT DID YOU HAVE TO SAY, OR THINK, OR IMAGINE? ALL THE SAME, IT WAS YOUR BOOK NOW. YOU COULD HEAR THE WIND COMING FROM HER MOUTH, OR WAS IT HER HANDS?

    I WILL BE WAITING FOR YOU HERE WHEN YOU ARRIVE, YOU BEGAN.... SUDDENLY REMEMBERING THE WORDS WRITTEN HOW MANY LIFETIMES BEFORE?

Koans
Book Two

SCROLL XV:

NO BIRTH / NO DEATH
    BEING OR NON BEING
  THIS DREAM YOU ONCE CLUNG TO
    ONCE CALLED THE NAME YOU
  YOU ARE EVERYTHING YOU ARE
    EVERYTHING
        YOU ARE NOT

THE IMPERMANENCE
OF IMPERMANENCE
IN THE ETERNAL NOW
OF THESE FACES OF GOD

I COULD HEAR YOU
    LAUGHING FROM THE SEA—
AND IF ANY THOUGHT
    ARISES FROM YOU
LET THE OLE FELLA KNOW...

SCROLL V:

Did he tell you the ghostwoman,
the silent one who writes your poetry,
who almost never spoke, dreams on
like the ringing of the monks' bells,
but you find it all in the poems
when you take them out of your
scrolls and read them again,
  hearing the bird again for
    the first time.

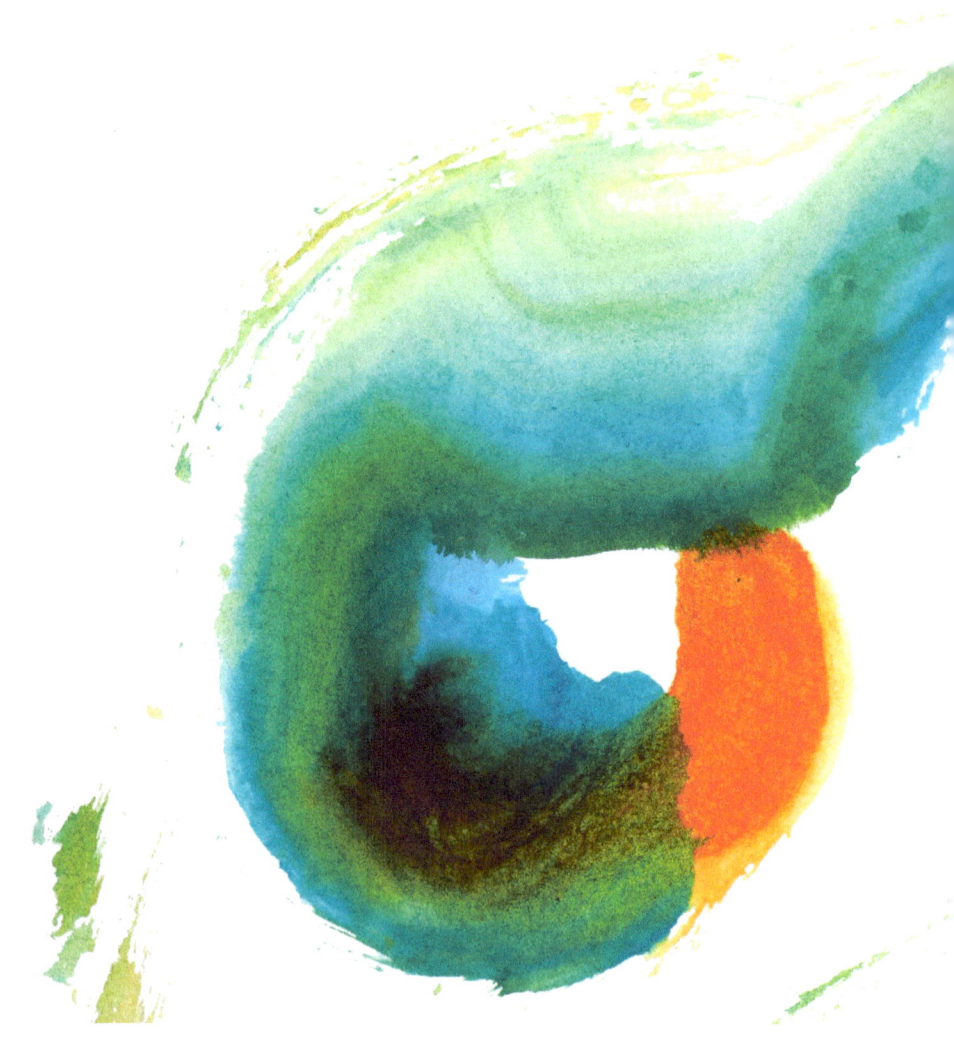

SCROLL VIII:

    THE DREAM IS LANGUAGE.
    THE MYSTERY IS THE OTHER.
    REALITY IS WAKING
              IN THIS MYSTERY.
   A BIRD IN FLIGHT.

SCROLL XVIII:

HOW DO WE ALL EXIST AT THE SAME TIME?

    THIS IS JUST YOU BECOMING YOU, AND YOU KNOW THIS. BY NOW, THE CLOUDS KNOW YOUR NAME. THE PAST & FUTURE EXIST IN THIS VERY MOMENT. BUT THERE IS THE PAST OF THE FUTURE, AND THE FUTURE OF THE PAST, THE PAST & FUTURE OF THE PRESENT, AND THE PAST & FUTURE OF THE FUTURE. WHY DO YOU THINK TIME IS SEPARATE FROM BEING STILL?

Acknowledgments

After doing a workshop with the great Japanese calligrapher, Kazuaki Tanahashi, I asked if he would paint an enso for my book. He stared at me for a long time. Then, he said—No, do it yourself. Thank you, Kaz.

About the Author

Zen monk and poet, Ninso John High, is the recipient of four Fulbrights and has been awarded two National Endowment for the Arts fellowships (fiction and translation) and a 2020 National Endowment for the Humanities for a translation project of Osip Mandelstam's *Voronezh Notebooks*. He is the author of numerous books of poetry, fiction, and translation—the most recent, *vanishing acts*, a work of cross-genre writings (Talisman House, 2018). A founder and former director of the LIU, Brooklyn MFA Program, he is currently on pilgrimage working with children, teachers, social workers, and writers, facilitating workshops in creative transformation in Cambodia, China, and Portugal.